THE RIGHT GIRL FOR ME

Keeping the right Person in the Relationship for Marriage.

Written by James Richard

TABLE OF CONTENTS

CHAPTER 1

INTRODUCTION.

There is no such thing as a perfect relationship. Even the most together couples have their disagreements. Look at Will Smith and Jada Pinkett-Smith! They're one of the most together couples in Hollywood, but even they had their rough patch. Because of this, it's often hard to know whether the person you're so taken with is the one or not.

If you're loved up but sometimes things don't go well, take heart in the fact that arguments and disagreements are normal. If anything, they're also healthy.

It's not good to constantly agree on everything, and healthy disagreements can help to develop the relationship to a higher level. However, if you're always bickering and you're wondering how to know if she is The One, that could be a sign that things aren't quite on track.

The best way to understand whether the girl you're dating is the right one for you or not is to know the real signs. However, also be aware that every couple, even the most together ones, have their ups and downs too.

«WHAT DOES IT MEAN TO BE THE ONE?
Before we delve into the signs for how to know if she is The One, let's first look at what it means. If someone is The One, it means that they're someone you could see yourself spending your life with. It doesn't mean there is only one single person for everyone on the planet, however.

Some people fall in love and are extremely compatible, but things happen and they go their separate ways over time. That person may then meet someone else and fall in love again but in a slightly different way.

For that reason, I don't believe there's only one person for everyone but I do believe that you can tell whether someone is serious future material by assessing your connection.

No relationship is ever the finished article, and there will always be challenges along the way. If you're able to come through them together and work as a team to make things better, that's the biggest and best sign there is.

SIGNS TO CHECK OUT IF SHE IS THE ONE.

There are so many signs to check out in your girlfriend that can prove to you whether both of you are meant to be together. Here I will shear with you different kind of signs which includes: signs that tell you she is the one, subtle signs she is not the one, signs a woman is pulling away from you, causes of women pulling away, and what you must do.

(1) YOU WANT TO SHARE EVERYTHING WITH HER.

This doesn't mean you're constantly going to spill the contents of your mind to her, but you want to share your thoughts and feelings with her, and she often does the same with you. When you meet The One, you don't want to hold things back.

(2) YOU SEE YOUR FUTURE WITH HER.

When learning how to know if she is The One, this is probably the biggest sign of them all. Do you see your future with her? If you can see yourselves together when you're old and grey, you're onto something good.

(3) SHE SUPPORTS YOU THROUGH THICK AND THIN.

A strong and supportive woman is the ideal life partner. She will be there for you through whatever life throws at you and always be your biggest cheerleader.

(4) YOU THINK SHE WOULD BE A GREAT LIFE PARTNER.

Not only do you see her in your future but you think she would make a great partner for life too.
How can you tell? She's not only supportive but she's also willing to work to make your relationship better. You can laugh together, you can cry together, and she's a partner in more than the usual sense.

(5) WHENEVER SOMETHING HAPPENS, SHE IS THE ONE YOU WANT TO TALK TO.

Good or bad, whenever something happens in your life, she's the one you want to reach out and speak to about it. You trust her advice and she always makes you feel better. How to know if she is the one? She's your trusted confidant.

(6) YOU ARGUE, BUT YOU WORK THROUGH IT.

Let's not kid ourselves and say that we're never going to argue or ever have disagreements because we will. However, those arguments don't last long and you're both willing to work through them to solve the problem. There are no grudges and no long periods of the silent treatment.

(7) YOU CAN COMMUNICATE WITH EACH OTHER EASILY.

How to know if she is the one comes down to so many elements but if you can communicate freely with each other and you don't feel embarrassed or worried to speak to her, you've met someone who understands you on a deeper level.

(8) SHE MAKES YOU WANT TO BE BETTER.

This is probably one of the biggest signs you've met The One. Being with her makes you want to do better and be better, for yourself and her. She makes you strive to meet your potential and be the best partner you can be.

(9) YOU WOULD DO ANYTHING TO MAKE HER SMILE.

Her smile brightens up your day and when she's happy, you're happy. Of course, when she's sad, it makes you feel down and off-kilter too. This isn't just about showing empathy, this is about having that strong connection.

(10) YOU CAN'T IMAGINE YOUR LIFE WITHOUT HER.

When you picture your life, she's in it and you can't imagine it being any other way. The sheer thought of her not around makes you feel down, sad, and perhaps even scared.

(11) YOU DIDN'T DREAM OF ANOTHER WOMAN.

This doesn't mean you're never going to find another woman attractive in your life, because that's unrealistic. But it means you'd never dream of doing anything about it because you'd never want to hurt her in that way. How to know if she is the one means committing yourself.

(12) SHE ACCEPTS EVERYTHING ABOUT YOU, GOOD AND BAD.

And of course, you do the same for her. Nobody is perfect and if she isn't concerned about your weaknesses and focuses more on your strengths, that means she's accepted you completely. It's a wonderful feeling.

(13) YOU ARE BOTH WILLING TO APOLOGIZE WHEN YOU ARE WRONG.

When two people aren't meant for each other, there is often pride standing in the way. That means if you're arguing, you're not going to want to apologize to make things better. If the opposite is true, she's possibly The One.

(14) YOU PUT EACH OTHER FIRST.

You want to make sure she's okay and she does the same for you. As a result, you always consider each other's feelings and you put one another first.

(15) YOUR FEELINGS GO BEYOND SEX.

At the start of a relationship, everything is passionate and it's all about bedroom time. As the relationship develops, of course, sex is still important but it's not all about that.

(16) LIFE IS BETTER WHEN SHE IS AROUND.

When she is around you, you feel calm and happy. Life is far more enjoyable when she is beside you and you're doing things together.

Of course, you can't be side by side 100% of the time, but when you are, things are great

(17) YOU ARE PARTNERS IN EVERYTHING.

How to know if she is The One? You're a team and you do the important things in life side by side, together, as a solid unit. That means you succeed and fail as one and you're always there for one another whenever needed.

CHAPTER 2

»SUBTLE SIGNS SHE IS NOT THE ONE.

You've learned how to determine whether she is The One, but what about signals that she's not the ideal one for you? These indications could be subtle, but they're strong you need to be alert of them. I have seen three years old marriages in which the Lady began acting weird, when inquiries were made the guy replied that she wasn't like that before. But the fact is that the indicators are always there from the beginning you are the one who decides to ignore it in the name of love or the thought that he would change later, forgetting that transformation takes a process. When your companion began misbehaving or doing some crazy things, it signifies that such a person had the character in them from the beginning. It was merely concealed from you, but if you take a closer look and examine it will be evident to you. This is one of the reasons why I usually counsel individuals not to go rush into sex once they have a new relationship, it will assist you to see through that person. Here are the symbols

(1) YOU REGULARLY MISUNDERSTAND EACH OTHER, AND COMMUNICATION IS DIFFICULT.

You find it hard to communicate and you frequently discover that you take things the wrong way or misinterpret one another. It just feels tough.

(2) SHE JUST DOESN'T GET YOU.

You get the impression of not being understood or accepted and there are aspects about her that you don't grasp fully either.

(3) IT'S OFTEN JUST ABOUT SEX.

If you remove sex out of the equation, what is left? That's a difficult question to answer and if you can't offer a clear response or you believe nothing remarkable would be left, that's a really strong warning.

(4) YOU DON'T HAVE A LOT IN COMMON.

Whilst opposites might occasionally attract, you do need a certain level of common ground. If you're struggling to discover it, you're going to struggle to understand each other.

(5) SHE REGULARLY CALLS OUT THE THINGS SHE DOESN'T LIKE ABOUT YOU.

It's not possible to adore everything about a person, but you can tolerate it. If she's not willing to do that, she's not The One.

(6) HER ECCENTRICITIES ARE A LITTLE ANNOYING TO YOU.

You're meant to find her peculiarities endearing and part of who she is, but if you simply find them bothersome, that's not the best indicator for longevity.

(7) YOUR VALUES DID NOT MATCH UP.

This is a significant issue. If your values aren't in harmony, your relationship is never going to make it. You may have slightly different values, but in the end, they have to line up in some manner.

(8) YOU BOTH WANT DIFFERENT THINGS.

Life is going to lead you down various routes in the end and that means you're going to confront heartache at some time in the future. When you both desire different things, you're either going to drift or one of you is going to have to concede much too much.

(9) WHEN YOU PICTURE THE FUTURE YOU ARE NOT SURE IF SHE IS IN IT.

That's fairly apparent, right? How to tell whether she is The One implies you see her in your future. If you visualize it and she's not there or you're not sure, things don't seem good. While you love someone, you will constantly remember them in all you do particularly when preparing. Once you realize that they have not been included, that's a red signal.

(10) YOU LOOK AT YOUR FRIENDS' RELATIONSHIPS AND FIND YOURS LACKING.

Firstly, never compare relationships but if you regularly feel that yours simply doesn't satisfy you in the same way that theirs appear to please them, you have to wonder why.

(11) YOU OFTEN FORGET THE SMALL THINGS ABOUT EACH OTHER.

Birthdays, middle names, preferred colors, and major milestones are all things that individuals remember about one another when they're linked. Sure, we occasionally forget but if it's frequent, it implies you're not paying attention for whatever reason.

(12) YOUR CONNECTION IS LACKING AND PEOPLE NOTICE IT.

People frequently tell you that you simply don't appear to be together and when you investigate it, you do feel that your connection isn't as strong as it might be. Do you work on it, or do you understand it's not meant to be?

(13) YOU OFTEN FIND YOURSELF DEFENDING YOUR RELATIONSHIP.

Your closest and dearest want the best for you and if they routinely express their worries about your relationship, you may find yourself continuously defending it consciously and subconsciously. Why is that?

(14) YOU DON'T HAVE LONG CONVERSATIONS.

Nobody wants to sit and have a full-on chat all the time. But if you can't recall the last time you did, you're not communicating properly.

(15) YOU OFTEN THINK ABOUT WHAT IT WILL BE LIKE IF YOU SPLIT UP.

It's not the greatest indicator if you constantly ponder what your life would be like if you broke up. If that's a regular feature, you're not involved.

«WHEN A WOMAN PULLS AWAY: WHY GIRLS DO IT? SIGNS AND WHAT YOU MUST DO.

When a lady pulls away, there is typically a very solid reason behind it. How to convince her to come back is difficult. Learning why females draw away is crucial. One of the most often googled queries regarding relationships on the internet is why men pull away, although women pull away in relationships just as often. When a woman pulls away, she does so for various reasons.

If you have a lady in your life who pulls away, the first step is to attempt to find out the reason. By doing so, you may identify the problem and try to address it. However, understanding why females draw away isn't always straightforward. Every woman is different, after all.

However, you know the lady in your life better than we do, so with a little insider information, you'll be able to uncover the problem and figure out what to do about it.

«THE SIGN A WOMAN IS PULLING AWAY FROM YOU.

Before we find out why she's drifting away from you, you need to detect the signals it's occurring. It's quite easy to confuse a few days of feeling worried and being distant because of it, with genuine pushing away. If you encounter several of these indicators, it might be that the lady in your life is attempting to create some considerable space between the two of you.

(1) SHE IS NONE COMMITTED WHEN YOU TRY TO MAKE PLANS.

We can't speak for all women, but most like making plans and going out to do something unusual with their significant other. When a woman draws away, she will become highly unbothered about establishing arrangements, particularly those that are too far in the distance.

(2) SHE IS NOT INTERESTED IN SEX.

Dips in libido can happen, so don't worry if your spouse has suddenly become a bit less interested in sex. Stress may have a major effect on how frequently someone feels like getting it on. However, if she's continually indifferent, it may be one of the indicators she's drifting away from you.

(3) SHE SEEMS TO BE SECRETIVE AND PREOCCUPIED.

This isn't a good thing. She isn't attempting to maintain a little mystery going on, which suggests she's probably paying her focus to someone else. If she's focused on work, that's fair enough, but if she's behaving a bit peculiarly and being secretive, she's pushing away from you and potentially attempting to move toward someone else.

(4) HER TEXT AND CALLS ARE BECOMING LESS FREQUENT.

And, it takes her longer to respond. This is one of the key indicators a lady is drifting away from you since it suggests she's not that interested in conversing.

Now, if this occurs once or twice, don't worry; she may simply be busy at work. But, if it's a frequent issue, you may want to rethink what's going on.

(5) SHE DOESN'T SEEM INTERESTED IN CONVERSATIONS OR WHAT YOU HAVE TO SAY.

At the start, things were perfect. You had a true connection, and you could have fantastic talks. Now, everything looks frigid, and it's as if she's erected a giant brick wall between the two of you. She's not interested since she's all in her thoughts. Finding out why ladies pull away is one thing, but viewing this as a huge indicator should come first.

(6) SHE SEEMS TO BE HANGING AROUND WITH DIFFERENT PEOPLE.

Do you have a shared group of friends, and she appears to be spending less and less time with the group? She's pushing away and going toward another group, seeking joy and conversation elsewhere.

CHAPTER 3
»CAUSES OF WOMEN PULLING AWAY, AND WHAT YOU MUST DO.

Women generally move away from a relationship due to unfairness, trust concerns, or questioning their emotions, but those aren't the only reasons. Learning why ladies pull away is a step in the correct path since it provides you with critical knowledge to continue. The problem? There are all kinds of reasons why women have drawbacks in a relationship. These are the most prevalent ones.

(1) YOU ARE NOT GIVING HER ENOUGH ATTENTION.

If you don't offer a lady enough attention, her immediate response can be to remove all the attention that she throws your way. Whether she continually dotes over you and you make her feel unimportant, she likely gets weary of your noncommittal conduct and pulls away to find out if you notice or care.

(2) SHE IS AFRAID OF COMMITMENT.

If she isn't ready to make a huge life commitment and believes it's headed that way, then she may simply want to take a step back and assess what it is that she wants out of the relationship. Contrary to what people generally assume, not every lady is worried about her biological clock or searching for the white picket fence and 2.5 kids. If she simply isn't quite ready to make it a "thing," she could attempt to create space to work things out in her thoughts.

(3) YOU ARE COMING ON TOO STRONG.

If you move too rapidly for her comfort, she may draw back. Women need to feel loved and needed. But, if you feel like you can't survive without her, grip on too tightly, or simply behave far too obsessively, then she could be attempting to create some space between the two of you. If you sense you may be traveling too quickly, calm down and let her catch up. Otherwise, you risk seeing her walk away. That's one of the key reasons why ladies turn away.

(4) SHE HAS BEEN HURT IN THE PAST.

The fear of loss and pain are two extremely potent motivators that drive relationship conduct. If she has been injured in the past, then it is probable she won't be too ready to plunge straight back into misery. No of the cause, if she suffered the pain of loss in her past, she draws back out of terror. Or, there can be a small voice inside of her that sends a danger signal to frighten her off.

(5) YOU SEND HER MIXED MESSAGES.

If you are really into her one minute but not the next, you give her mixed signals. Perhaps you shrink back from her and don't even notice it. Sometimes we draw out from individuals without even noticing until they do the same. It doesn't feel nice to be on the receiving end. So, when a lady pulls back, assess the way you act to ensure you show her how you feel, or you could just lose her.

(6) SHE IS UNSURE OF HER FEELINGS.

Don't stress out. She could be unclear about how she feels about you and your future with you. When things grow serious, it is not that unusual for individuals to second guess what they feel, and takes some time to straighten things out in their brains. If she pulls back, allow her the room to figure out what it is she wants. You don't want to push her to decide or put pressure on her. The only way to be sure things will turn out the way they should, is to allow her the breathing space to acquire some perspective.

(7) SHE DOESN'T TRUST YOU.

If you are a Romeo who can't stop following or being followed by your harem of ladies on social media, she probably doesn't trust you. Whether you cheated on an ex, can't let go of your ex, or can't stop flirting with other females, something warns her not to become too involved. This is one of the key reasons why ladies draw away, so assess what you do that may push her from you.

(8) SHE DOESN'T THINK YOU ARE INTO HER.

No one likes to be rejected. If you act far less into her than she is into you, or appear not to be that involved, then she will follow suit.

Playing hard to get only works initially, and after a time, it becomes your relationship's deadliest adversary. At some time, let your defenses down and leave yourself exposed. If not, there is a probability she'll draw back and quit attempting to like you more than she believes you like her.

(9) SHE ISN'T OVER THE PREVIOUS RELATIONSHIP.

If she began dating you too early following the split from someone crucial in her life, she isn't over her former relationship. Sometimes there are lingering sentiments that you don't even identify until you become close to someone else. At that time, you know that it isn't quite right. If she hasn't let go of someone in her past, she pulls back to find out which connection is genuine and what it is that she wants before she is all in.

(10) SOMETHING JUST DOESN'T FEEL RIGHT.

There are moments in a relationship when things simply don't seem right. No of the reason, if that inner voice tells her things are awry, she's taking the time to stand back and uncover the root of her fear and tension in your relationship. Give her time to find out why she doesn't feel as if it is a match made in heaven for both of your sakes.

(11) YOU ARE TOO AGGRESSIVE.

You're too much and not in a good way. You're too much in her face, too lovey-dovey, simply too much. This isn't horrible, but for her, it's overwhelming. Take it easy, cowboy. Your assertiveness is leading her to freak out and withdraw. If you desire her, it's okay, but don't make her feel like she's being chased.

(12) SHE IS SCARED.

Falling in love is a huge thing. It's scary. People fall in love and are rejected, and it might be weighing hard on her mind. Some individuals take longer to examine their emotions and determine whether it's for them or not. So, maybe she truly likes you, but she's terrified right now. Don't push her, give her room, and speak to her. If she's terrified, she'll tell you what she needs from you.

(13) SHE IS NOT THAT INTO YOU.

She went on a few dates with you and tried it out, but she's not into you like that. Sure, she thinks you're kind and a wonderful person, but for her, you're lacking something. You're simply not for her and that's why she's pushing away.

(14) YOU ARE IMPATIENT AND NOT ENJOYING THE MOMENT.

One of the greatest reasons why ladies pull away is because you're pushing things too rapidly. She likes you, and you like her, but you're already searching for the ring, and it's just the second date. You need to slow things down and take a breath. If you're overly impatient, she'll sense it, and it makes a woman uncomfortable very quickly. Too, just try to enjoy the moment; even if you desire a future with her, don't make it so clear just now.

(15) SHE IS SUFFERING FROM FOMO.

Or, sometimes known as the "fear of missing out." She likes you, but she's also interested in the man who works at Starbucks. Do you understand what we mean? She doesn't want to commit to you because she's not ready to stop seeing other people. You're too serious for her, and she still wants to play the field. This doesn't mean she doesn't like you, she does, just not enough.

(16) YOU ARE BECOMING SOFT.

Now, we don't believe you should become an asshole to attempt to retain her, this isn't what it's about. But she enjoyed the pursuit, and she liked that you didn't always give her what she wanted. Now, you're in love with her, and you want to do nothing more than shower her with presents, we understand it. But don't do it. Treat her properly and treat her with respect but don't throw up the towel and abandon yourself to her. She may be bored now that she's getting her way all the time.

(17) YOU ARE NOT GIVING HER THE SPACE SHE NEEDS.

You see that she's drifting away. Instead of conversing with her or giving her space, you suffocate her. Look, we understand it. You're frightened of losing her, so you attempt to bring her back to you. But, by smothering her, you won't get her back. You need to give her the space she needs as she's already in her mind with contemplation. Instead of getting in her face, chat with her.

CHAPTER 4
»WHAT SHOULD YOU DO WHEN A WOMAN PULLS AWAY FROM YOU.?

You know the signals, and you know the reasons why ladies draw away, but what should you do about it? The main line is that you can't compel someone to stay around simply because you want them to. That's the greatest trouble with love — we can't always have what, and who, we desire.

But, if you're finding that she's slipping away from you, don't despair just yet. There might yet be hope. The first thing to do is make sure that this is truly occurring. Are you putting two and two together and getting twenty? Check out our collection of signs and see how many you can nod along to. If you have many, it's quite probable you have a problem. If it's only one or two and it's only periodically, calms a bit.

The next step is to attempt and speak to her. Don't make this a major, formal talk. Just say something like, "is everything okay? I've simply noticed you've been distant recently. It might be that she's anxious to speak about it, but she's terrified to make the first step.

If she insists everything is good, give her some space. Allow her the time she needs to work things out. It might be that it's all she truly wants. But if nothing changes, you have to look at the notion that maybe she doesn't want to be in this relationship after all.

«NOBODY SAID LOVE WAS EASY.

Typically, when a man pulls back, it is because he doesn't sure what he feels. When a woman pulls back, she probably does and attempts to reconcile what concerns her or what she wants to accomplish moving ahead. Learning why ladies draw away may benefit you to an extent.

The worst thing to do in any relationship when someone pulls away is to press them to make a choice soon. Give them the breathing space to determine what they want. If you don't, you face the genuine danger of losing them.

Don't ever pursue somebody who isn't playing tag. When a lady pulls away, she will tell you what's going on when she is ready. Give her the time to explain.

www.ingramcontent.com/pod-product-compliance
Lightning Source LLC
LaVergne TN
LVHW020536160826
845677LV00015B/4089